The Conflict Resolution Library™

Dealing with Feeling Left Out

• Don Middleton •

The Rosen Publishing Group's
PowerKids Press™
New York

This book is dedicated to my wife, Sue; my daughters, Jody and Kim; my mother-in-law, Mim; and my parents, Bernice and Helmut Bischoff. Also, special thanks to authors and friends Diana Star Helmer and Tom Owens for believing in me. —Don Middleton

Published in 1999 by The Rosen Publishing Group, Inc.
29 East 21st Street, New York, NY 10010

Photo Credits and Photo Illustrations: pp. 4, 7 © Ron Maratea/International Stock; pp. 8, 11 by Seth Dinnerman; p. 12 © George Ancona/International Stock; p. 15 © Jeremy Scott/ International Stock; p. 16 by Maria Moreno; p. 19 © Scott Campbell/International Stock; p. 20 © Phyllis Picardi/International Stock.

First Edition

Layout and design: Erin McKenna

Middleton, Don.
    Dealing with feeling left out / by Don Middleton.
        p.   cm.—(The conflict resolution library)
    Includes index.
    Summary: Describes how it feels to be excluded, why this might happen, and how to handle such situations.
    ISBN 0-8239-5269-X
    1. Social isolation—Juvenile literature. [1. Social isolation. 2. Interpersonal relations.] I. Title. II. Series.
    HM291.M465 1998
    302.5'45—dc21   98-5642
                                                                                                  CIP
                                                                                                   AC

Manufactured in the United States of America

Contents

Feeling Left Out

We feel a lot of **emotions** (ee-MOH-shunz), such as happiness or sadness, each day. How other people act toward us can affect how we feel. Sometimes we feel **excluded** (eks-KLOO-ded), or left out. It doesn't feel good to be left out. When we feel left out, we often have other feelings, such as hurt or **disappointment** (dis-uh-POYNT-ment). We may also feel anger toward others for not including us. Everybody has felt left out. But there are things we can do to deal with these feelings.

◀ *Feeling left out can make us sad.*

Belonging

Each of us wants others to like us and care about us. We want to belong. Every day, your parents show how they care about you. At school, your teachers and classmates work and play with you. Outside of school, you and your friends hang out together. All of these things help us feel that we belong. The key to belonging is making sure others feel that they also belong. One way to do this is to invite other kids to take part in **activities** (ak-TIH-vih-teez) with you.

Talking to your teacher can help you feel like you belong in your class. ▶

The New Girl

Jennifer and Kyra were eating in the lunchroom. "There's Louise, the new girl who just moved to the neighborhood," said Jennifer.

"She's sitting all alone. Let's ask her to sit with us," said Kyra.

"Good idea. I'll go ask her," Jennifer said as she hurried to Louise's table.

Soon the three girls were talking and having fun.

"Thanks for including me. Eating alone isn't any fun," Louise said.

◀ *Including another person can give both of you a sense of belonging.*

Look at Yourself

Anyone who has ever felt left out may wonder, Why me? Sometimes the answers are easy to find. Maybe you always want to have your way when you play with others. Or you might have said mean things about someone in front of other kids. Perhaps your friends don't think you have anything nice to say about anyone else. It is important to be kind to others and to try to get along with different people. When you do, people will be more interested in spending time with you.

If you've been left out of something, take some time to think about why you've been left out. ▶

Take a Chance

There have been times when each of us has been afraid to take a chance. What if your school is having tryouts for a sports team? Or a teacher asks someone to be class reporter on the school newspaper? Maybe your parents want to know if you'll help at the neighborhood picnic. Jump right in! The more activities you get involved in, the less time you'll have to sit around and feel left out. You'll also have fun and meet a lot of people.

◀ *If you're feeling left out in school, try raising your hand to ask questions. Or you might volunteer if your teacher asks someone to speak to the rest of the class.*

Baseball Tryouts

John and Chris were trying out for the school baseball team.

"I hope we both make the team," said John.

"You'll make it! You play so well," said Chris.

"You're getting better too," John said.

"Even if I don't make it, I've learned a lot and made friends during the tryouts," said Chris.

After the tryouts, John asked Chris, "Even though you didn't make the team, will you still come to games?"

"Sure. Now I'm friends with everybody on the team," Chris said.

Playing on or rooting for a sports team can make you feel like you belong to a group. ▶

Be a Leader

Some kids always wait for others to ask them to do things. Why sit back and wait? Take the **initiative** (ih-NIH-shuh-tiv). You can arrange with your friends to play together after school. You can plan games to play during recess by talking before class starts in the morning. By being a leader, you help make sure fun activities get organized. That way, you make sure everyone, including you, gets to be part of the fun.

◀ *Meet up with friends before school to think up fun group activities.*

Lead by Example

Some kids form groups that other kids can't join. A bunch of boys may not let anyone else sit at their lunch table. A group of girls might run away when other classmates try to join them on the playground.

Lead by example! Don't join any group that other kids can't join. Try to be a friend to everyone. From your actions, other kids might see how good it is to include everybody.

Make the effort to include everyone in your activities. ▶

The New Student

Cameron and Nora were talking about the new boy in school.

"I've never known anyone in a wheelchair," Nora said.

"Neither have I, but he seems nice," Cameron said.

"I wonder if he plays sports," Nora said.

"Why not ask him?" Cameron asked.

Later, Nora told Cameron, "The new boy's name is Samuel. He plays wheelchair sports. I asked him to sit with us at the library tomorrow."

◀ *Everyone enjoys joining in the fun!*

The Challenge

Knowing some of the things you can do to avoid feeling left out can help you through tough **situations** (sih-choo-AY-shunz). Sometimes making new friends can be scary. And it takes time and effort to include everybody in the games you and your friends play. It can be a challenge to make sure nobody feels left out. But having a lot of people share in the fun makes things even more fun. New friends can make an old game seem new again!

Glossary

activity (ak-TIH-vih-tee) Something you do for fun.

disappointment (dis-uh-POYNT-ment) A feeling of being let down.

emotion (ee-MOH-shun) A feeling.

exclude (eks-KLOOD) To prevent someone from joining a group or activity.

initiative (ih-NIH-shuh-tiv) The first step toward doing something.

situation (sih-choo-AY-shun) A problem or event.

Index